Stealing Flowers from the Neighbors

Sherw Levine

Stealing Flowers from the Neighbors

Poems by

Sherri Levine

Cover design by Shay Culligan
Cover painting *Rose Trio* by Kay Levine

ISBN: 978-1-63980-010-0

Kelsay Books
502 South 1040 East, A-119
American Fork, Utah 84003
Kelsaybooks.com

In memory of my mother, Kay Levine

Acknowledgments

My sincere appreciation goes to the editors at these publications in which the following poems appeared:

CALYX : "Girl," "Facedown"

CIRQUE: "Gold Star"

Clackamas River Review: "Where My Father Stands," "When I Wouldn't Eat My Disgusting Liver"

Chrysalis Poem Anthology: "Swimming in the Rain"

Driftwood Press: "I Remember Not Sleeping"

Hartskill Review: "Orange Crush"

Jewish Literary Journal: "Taharah," "Through the Window at the Hospice Center," "Camellia's Bloom"

Mizmor Anthology: "Lilacs"

Mom Egg: "Questions for the Hospice Nurse"

The Opiate: "Weekend Call to My Father," "I Ate a Raymond Carver," "Dear Albania," "The Man Next Door"

/pãn| dé| mïk/ 2020: An Anthology of Pandemic Poems: "Through the Window at the Hospice Center"

Poeming Pigeon: "There is Poetry in These Rooms," "Aunt Sylvia's Eyebrows"

Poet Lore: "The Angel in the Isolation Room"

Postcard Poems: "Tiny Buds"

Red Coyote Journal: "Tell Me What It's Like"

Timberline Review: "Grammar Lessons"

U.S. 1 Worksheets: "A Million Stars"

Verseweavers: "Don't Bother the Flowers," "Stealing Flowers from the Neighbors"

VoiceCatcher: A Journal of Women's Voices & Visions: "She Steps Out of His Pickup Truck," "Girl"

The Voices Project: "The Brightest Stars"

Willawaw Journal: "Sunday Morning," "A Kind of Disaster," "Swimming in the Rain," "Drug Clinic"

Worcester Review: "Anniversary," "Remembering Her Less," "Unleashed"

And a very special thanks to the judges of the following contests: "Facedown" won the 2019 Lois Cranston Memorial Poetry Prize, "Don't Bother the Flowers" won First Place (Poet's Choice), Oregon Poetry Association Fall Poetry Contest (2017), "Stealing Flowers from the Neighbors" won Second Place (Members Only), Oregon Poetry Association Spring Poetry Contest (2020).

Special Thanks

Special thanks to: John Sibley Williams, my editor and mentor; my teachers Andrea Hollander, John Morrison, and Penelope Scambly Schott. I am grateful to Dale Champlin and Anne Farley for their unwavering support and encouragement; to the Prosperity Pie Poets and our incredible poetry community; to Scott Snedecor and Cristina Prado, who are with me in spirit; to Bob and Adrian for their patience, compassion, and kindness; to my mother, Kay Levine, who always believed in me.

Contents

You have to keep breaking your heart until it opens
—Rumi

There Is Poetry in These Rooms

There is poetry in these rooms,
in the folds of our sheets,
the sweat of your brow,
the ease of language,
of what we say, and what we don't say.
It's the crease of your skin,
paper thin and smooth,
like a letter pressed
between pages of an old book.
It's a musty kiss,
tossed chips under the bed
with dust and magazines.
It's the taste of salt on your neck,
our morning breath,
the sprouts you still call hair.
It's the yipping of the neighbor's dogs,
creaking and moaning floors.
It's the streetlight that shines
through our blinds
we call our moon.

Girl

The Brightest Stars

Tonight, the sky's a picture box
where stars that pulse and pulsate
are like fireflies my sister and I
tried to catch, but couldn't keep
in our hands long enough to put in jars
and carry them like lanterns in a storm.
We would wait for the darkness
where bats that looked like birds
would rise from our tree
flitter, flutter, flying far away.
When dishes smacked against
kitchen walls and blinds slammed shut
we knew we had to go somewhere
we could not know.
Our navigators:
Streetlamps
The brightest stars
A steady white moon.

A Kind of Disaster

I've known earthquakes in my home
pots being thrown, plates crashing into
one another, drapes closing
in the afternoon.
I've felt the boom! boom!
above my bed
and watched my dolls shake
their heads.
I don't know what it must have felt like
afterwards,
what *she* must have felt.
I never got to see her
exhausted
mess
on
the
floor.
Still
I lay there
waiting
for something to happen,
or change—
for her to come and get me
so I could hold her.

Sunday Mornings

My mother drags the rugs out
of our red brick house, one-by-one
down the steps, in front of the neighbors.
She beats the rugs with her broom
as if they are flesh-eating aliens.
I want to scream, "No!" "Stop!"
but all I can do is cover my face
with my hands. I smell my breath—
maple syrup, challah, sour milk.
If only I had a stick of peppermint gum,
everything would be a lot of better.

Facedown

He untucks his shirt
pulls down his zipper
pushes my head on his lap.
To me, it looked like the neon pink
monster sea worm
I once saw in a magazine.
Penis worm, they called it,
undulating at the bottom of the sea,
its dimple-eyed body pulsated
like my mother's twisted
blue veins.
What would it be like
to float on the surface,
facedown, without sinking?
Arms loose and long,
would I hear the sound
of my heart beating?
Now, with my head still pressed
down by his football hands,
I'm swimming laps
at the Y,
stretching one arm,
then the next,
each breath no different
than the one
that carries me
to the other side.

Girl

steps out
of the subway
in her shimmy
shine short shorts
shoe-fly
halter tie
crop top—
she thinks of last night
with the boy
in
her
hands.
Ooooh la la
so magnifique
he says for her to call
him but the phone
is B-R-O-K-E
the ticket window just
C-L-O-S-E-D
She knows if she runs
past the sticky-stank
double dip dumb
fuckers
their hands
on a girl's
breasts
up her skirt
inside her mouth—
She knows she can
make it past

the E-M-E-R-G-E-N-C-Y signs
for the boy in the park
who waits for her
in the dark.

She Steps Out of His Pick-Up Truck

She steps out of his pickup truck
into the blue of the day,
somewhere west, south
where geese fly in formation,
hearts wrapped around their compass.
She breathes in deep,
once, then again,
sighs heavily,
tingling with the memory
of the stranger in the truck—
gentle, generous, kind,
cacophony of uhs and ohs,
crescendoed bliss.
Curt farewells
kiss on the cheek
the door slammed shut.
She presses the button of the elevator,
opens her apartment door,
thinks of all the possibilities
of hope and the open road.
The dimly lit
papier mache star
hanging on the ceiling,
guides her home
to a nesting place,
her heart wrapped around
the steering wheel.

Tiny Buds

When my mother finds two bumps
on my nine-year-old chest,
she screams *"Cancer!"*
Under my gown,
the doctor's freezing hands
pinch and squeeze.
He kneads my flesh like pink putty.
With clenched toes,
I scream, "Ouwee!"
Patting me on my shoulder,
the doctor tells me,
"You don't have cancer.
You are going through puberty,"
as though I had just won a prize.

Aunt Sylvia's Eyebrows

I wish I could tingle
like a spin-the bottle-kiss,
have 7 minutes of *Heaven*
in the Closet with Charlie or Jim.
Should I speak French
when I French kiss them?
I wish I had my sisters' big boobs,
her lime green string bikini,
the blond highlights
she makes from squeezing lemons
into her ash brown hair.
For hours, she stands in front of the bathroom mirror
flipping her Farrah Fawcett feathers.
I lie in her messy bed, thinking about
my visit to Aunt Sylvia's.
We stood at the patio window
and watched a gray squirrel
chase another squirrel across the yard,
up a tree, along the fence, on the roof,
their eyes wide, ears pricked.
"Sweetheart," Aunt Sylvia said.
She pointed her long pastel pink fingernail
to the squirrels and squeezed
my arm. She said, "Boys won't want you if
you're too easy." Her dark eyebrows scrunched
up like a wooly bear.

End of the World

It was the end of the world in Mrs. Wallace's third grade class.
      I spilled milk on my green corduroy jumper dress. She
told me to leave the room and scrub my body clean.

While swinging in Damien Potter's backyard,
      he pointed to the tufts of hair under my arms,
and screamed, *Ewe!*

It was the end of the world when Chuckie "Cheese" Henderson
      dumped me because I refused to lie on the crusted-over
snow,
his freezing hands roaming under my thermals.

Back home, Aunt Harriet put her arm around my shoulder,
      softly said,
"Honey, some day you will look back, and these people won't
      mean anything."

Now that you are gone, Mom, I know she wasn't talking about
you.
      I see you standing there, bundled in fleece, at the top of my
street.

You are waving, waiting for me to leave, to reach my house,
      but you were already gone.

Swimming in the Rain

With my hands on her still strong shoulders,
I steer my mother
to the discount rack,
so she won't complain
about the prices.
The salesgirl comes over
wearing an Oregon Ducks T-shirt,
her smart phone squeezed
into the back pocket
of her rhinestone jeans.
Cracking her gum, she asks
my mother in slow motion,
CAN-I-HELP-YOU?
My mother is slow as rain,
a creaky, twisted
bicycle chain.
Back at the car, she lifts
the black bathing suit
and folds it neatly on her lap.
"I look like a fat seal in that thing,"
she says, and I tell her,
"And I'm a seagull
crashing into the surf."
It's been raining
for hours
both of us swimming now
in uncharted waters.

Astral Body

Before my mother woke up,
before scrambled eggs
and mandelbread,
before *Soul Train*
boogied on the TV, before
cats fought with chickens
on the fire escape, before
dirty diesel wafted
from streets below,
Before Count Basie and Ellington,
Mr. Cavallari's whiskers fell
into the sink, before a slap on the
wrist or on the behind.
Before clouds shrouded the sky,
turning everything into a permanent gray.
When white stripes broke the blue sky
in twos or fours.
Soon, my mother would shout
from the shower:
"Get to the kitchen, now!"
I'd drag my chair close
to the stove and count 29 bubbles
of her avocado poly coffee pot.
I was mesmerized by the starburst
design on its front,
how its silver rays cast
light into the sky,
my astral body
rising like steam.

I Ate a Raymond Carver

I ate a Raymond Carver
at the Press Club Café
It tasted good: smoked salmon, spinach
tomato, shallots, fresh dill.

If I ate you,
Raymond Carver,
would I write like you?
Minimal, genuine, chiseling
flesh-and-blood characters:
living, struggling, working,
always longing for something or
someone.

I'd like to hold a blind man's
hand, draw a cathedral,
throw all my furniture on the
lawn, or peer through a locked
door, like a hungry,
horny neighbor.

I long for someone
I can touch
but cannot hold.
I wonder if I write like you,
Raymond Carver, would I
die a cancerous death?

I reach for a cigarette
and feel despair.

I think I'll take a bite of Henry Miller
and Anais Nin:
Nutella, candied nuts, whipped cream.

First Date, or Flaming Cheese

At the Greek place
on West Burnside,
our first date.
Not even yet of drinking age,
you order the wine.
I study your profile,
thick black curls, long eyelashes,
ears like dried apricots.
We watch the belly dancer's
beaded breasts. Her shoulders shimmy,
sequined hips drop and lift.
The waiter with the hawk nose
carries a plate of golden cheese,
douses it with ouzo. Its heavenly wings
ablaze. He shouts, "Opa!" We shout, "Opa!"
The whole place shouts, "Opa!"

Salton Sea in G Minor

the man I love
jumps from my bed
like a spooked fish

he skims the surface
of my river
hungry for bugs
sustenance love

the man I love
drowns his sorrows
in ink

he drinks to write
like Hemmingway
or Burroughs

he doesn't bathe
change his clothes
brush his teeth

he stinks like hundreds of dead fish
beached by the Salton Sea

their bones turn to shells
I could pick my teeth with

Once

after Cecilia Woloch

Weren't we standing there once,
gripping the walls, pulling off shirts,
unsnapping straps, rustling up the sheets,
and weren't we naked and fragile and young?
Weren't you the hum and I the mum,
But didn't we know it wouldn't all turn out,
And weren't we just standing there once?

Birthday Gift

after Marc Chagall

Above the kissing couple hovering
over the smoker's table,
the dog dreaming on the rug,
simmering pot of mushroom barley soup,
above the radio's crackling static,
the neighbor's high-pitched clarinet,
madam singing libretto,
her emerald gown fading
in the closet,
above steam rising from the radiator,
metal pipes banging,
mother's iron hissing
on our damp underwear,
her trilling tongue rolled up
like a sausage bun.
Above birdless heaven,
the town emptied of row houses,
churches, herds of lazy cows.
The lonely cloud moves
across air as dust.
Below, moon glow
casts shafts of light
on two lovers
who toss birds
and flowers
into the sky.

Anniversary

Pillowing around
your belly hung, hair
less arm, white
knuckled, gripping
cleaned cotton sheets.
Pity, I should leave
the shelter of this
prideful den,
bursting, bright
camellia bloom,
wisps of hair falling
on slow pillows,
whimpering in your one
good ear, we tousle
and turn, twining my arms
and legs around your faithful
neck, like vines climbing
our backyard tree,
winded and worn,
baby it's cold outside.
Kiss the snow
from my lips
come hold
my heart
in your hands.

When I Wouldn't Eat My Disgusting Liver

When I wouldn't eat my disgusting
liver my mother said I should be
grateful. "Children are starving in
Africa," she'd say, dumping more
ketchup on my plate. When I was
sick and wanted broth, my mother
told me it could be worse; I might be
dying of diphtheria. "You should be
grateful you have your health."

When my husband left, she said
she never really liked him, that he
was way too young for me.
I watched her pull back her wrinkles,
sighing into the rearview mirror.
"Look, you should be grateful that you are
still young and pretty. I remember when
you were a little girl you used to dance
in front of the stove; you looked so happy—
When I started losing my looks she said,
"Be grateful at least you have your legs."
Recently, I lost my job. "A slap in the face,"
she said. "Well, at least you have your
teeth," she said, pointing to her
implants— "These cost a fortune."

The Man Next Door

The man next door vacuums in the nude.
I can see him from our adjoining balconies

high above the street. He pulls down the bed,
lies against the wall, turns on the news, and jerks off.

At least, I think that's what he's doing.
It's hard to get anything done.

On the kitchen table, my students' unmarked papers pile up.
I haven't once thought of my ex-husband's

new home in Chicago. I feel relieved
I won't have to see him again.

Last year at the airport,
I stood at the gate waiting to board my plane

when I thought I saw him holding hands
on the movable walkway with his wife and baby.

"Divorce is worse than death," my lawyer said
when she handed me the papers to sign.

"Worse," she said with a little laugh, "because he is still alive."
In the closet, I look for my black hoodie and dark sunglass.

To see him, I have to climb over
the balcony, crank my neck, but now

his lights are out. Below, the street sounds
are ocean waves, crashing.

Grammar Lessons

When my students ask me how to use the future tense,
I tell them we use *will* for a promise or a threat.
I *will* always love you, for example.
And to make a plan, we use the *present continuous,*
I *am divorcing* him.
When they ask about the *simple past,*
He *loved* me a long time ago . . .
It's not that simple, I tell them.
There's certainly nothing perfect about the *present perfect,*
I *have loved* you since the day I met you.
I ask them, does this mean he stopped loving me?
But *loving* is a *non-continuous verb,*
Loving, I tell them, is incorrect.
And for the *modals*?
(Though confused, I know I still have their interest)
I may, I might, I should, I could
keep going, but I won't
Instead, I tell them:
Love is full of tenses.

Swindler

I present this poem to you—
a hidden message stuck
under a postage stamp,
a salesman in a trench coat
slotted with Rolex watches,
a shell and pea street scam,
bouquets of crumpled paper flowers,
a moonlit carriage ride through Central Park
with a headless horseman.
I offer this poem to you—
a giant inflatable Mickey Mouse escort
holding my small hand through
the Macy's Day overflowing parade.
He takes our photograph
then turns around and asks
me to pay for it.

Orange Crush

I saw my man
put a dollar
in the soda machine
to buy a Coke
but the Coke didn't come out
instead what came out
was an Orange Crush.
My man was banging that machine
so hard with his fists
yelling—
Goddamn it! Goddamn machine!
but when he got the Orange Crush
he drank it anyway.
Why? I asked him.
Cause it's here
and I'm thirsty
You get used to it—
You get used to a lot of things, he said.
I'll never get used to losing you,
I told him.

Weekend Call to My Father

When my father can't lift his wife
off the kitchen floor, he calls the fire department.
"They come so often to the house," he says on the phone.
"I buy them boxes of doughnuts."
He coughs a few times, clears his throat,
then blows his nose.
I can picture him, sitting on his cracked blue
leather chair, newspapers strewn
over the worn carpet.

I used to watch my father talk to himself,
his shoulders shrugged as he pulled
his eyebrows, hands moved as if
he was shooing flies.
In our musty garage, his punching bag
hanging from the ceiling,
I once stood next to him, while he fixed his car.
Hands covered in oil, he yelled out,
"Screwdriver!" but when I gave him
the wrong one, his bald head pulsated bright red.

He asks, "Do you need any money?"
He's pressing cherry tobacco
into his pipe, cracking pine nuts with his teeth,
his stocks rising and falling on the TV.
I need to get off the phone.
I haven't even had my first cup of coffee.
But now, he's the one who has to go,
his wife's calling him from somewhere
in the house, somewhere I hope
he can get to
in time.

Where My Father Stands

I'm standing in the yard
holding a rake. My
father calls my name,
"Come here," he says.
With the tip of his pipe,
he points to a stack of
paper bags and gloves
lying on the garage
shelf. I'm afraid to go
inside the garage; I
might trip and fall on
the cracks, and get
bitten by a recluse.
"Don't kill the spiders,
my father says, "they eat
insects for lunch."
I don't know how I'm
going to fit all those
leaves into the paper
bags. A warm wind picks
up. A whirlwind of
dust and willow leaves
twirl until they drop.
I ask my father if
he's ever seen leaves
dance like that? I turn to
see if he's watching.
He's already gone.

Gold Star

I sprint down my street
as if I just discovered light
after being lost
in a cave for weeks.
I tell my mother
that a man wearing
a black leather jacket
rolled down his car window
and told me to climb in.
I tell this to the policeman
taking notes from our blue
plastic-covered couch.
"Do you remember what his car
looked like or the number
on his license plate?"
I bite my lip until it bleeds.
I grip my knees
and count all six points
on the gold star pinned
to his shirt pocket.
He scribbles something
I cannot see
in his little book,
stuffs it into his back pocket,
gets up to leave.
Outside, I hear kids still
playing wiffleball
in the street.

Across the Tappan Zee Bridge

In my mother's brand-new Camaro,
we putter along in our lane.

Cars honk and trucks shout.
She cranks up the radio, singing

with Bob Seger. Windows down,
I watch her tinted blue hair dance wildly

in the breeze. Every car that dares to pass,
I shoot with my imaginary gun.

I don't blame my mother for driving so slowly,
for the long trips to visit my grandfather.

I don't blame her for coming home
late when I was afraid to be alone.

I don't blame her not being able to find a job,
or keep one. For feeding me cottage cheese

and ginger ale for supper. Back home
I lie safely back into her soft lap

on her rocking chair.
Silently, she unties the ribbons

from my ponytail, brushes my hair until
it falls down my shoulders.

The Greatest Jewish Cowboy

My grandfather covered me in his arms with his old wool coat, too itchy for me, too warm to complain. I could never complain of the stories my grandfather whispered in my ear—the good guys, the bad guys—the Nazis.

While his distressed eggs cracked inside the covered pot, the tea kettle whistled like a tightly packed train, cats fought with chickens on the fire escape, an old shoe held the window open just enough to keep out the snow.

I imagined my grandfather in his cowboy hat and snakeskin boots riding his horse through the desert, shooting at scorpions, spiders, and rattlesnakes, calling out *yee-haw*. I listened to his voice echo through the canyon while lightning split open the sky.

I saw my grandfather catch the Nazis crawling out from under the rocks. He lassoed their necks, roped their arms and legs, and branded them with a red-hot iron. Then he dragged those fuckers into the shed. Someone lit a match, and everyone danced around the fire.

He'd laugh and laugh . . .

My grandfather died while I slept. I wanted more stories, for him to pinch my cheek and say my name. I wanted him to tell me that everything would be okay before he rode away.

Old Wool Coat

Seated on his favorite brown leather chair, Grandpa Morris counts coins from the pocket. "This army coat, he says, "is the coat two hoboes used to cover my frostbitten body. After the explosion hit the river, they found me floating in shallow water under the bridge. They dragged my frozen blue body onto the riverbank and scurried like mice back to their tents. When my army buddies saw my body on the ground, they took me for a carcass recently dropped from the back of passing morgue truck and carried my stiff body to the crematorium."

Grandpa Morris bends his contorted body to kiss the top of my frizzy brown hair. I hear stones crunch between his teeth. His wool coat smells like a dark basement, his breath like yeast. Before he hugs me goodbye, he wraps his coat around his shoulders, like a cape, holds in open. "C'mon," he says. "Get in."

Hothouse

On top of the fridge, the transistor
radio croons *Careless Love.*
My grandmother plunks the whole chicken
into the pot, heats the water to a rolling boil,
skims a layer of yellow fat with a spoon,
simmers the soup until late Sunday afternoon.

All the windows in the house fog;
my grandma's reading glasses too.
She wears them for chopping onions.
I see her wipe burning tears from her face
with the tissue she stuffs into her bra.

The whole house reeks of garlic, paprika.
The sweet smell of parsley and parsnips
permeates my newly Prelled hair.
I can even smell it on the glistening folds
of my grandmother's skin.

She's four and a half feet tall,
silver poufy hair,
lipstick the color of an eggplant.
In her lavender house robe,
she hunches over the soup, her lemon
yellow phone pushed against her ear.
The curly-Q cord stretches from the hall
to the stove. She presses her shrugging
shoulder against the telephone receiver,
gossips with her *yenta* friends. I cannot

believe the phone cord does not
rip out of the wall,
the way she pulls and twists,
wrapping it around her tiny wrist.

Don't Bother the Flowers

When grandma told me
to stop buying her flowers
I didn't know what to do
with the daffodils
I was holding in my hand.
Should I throw them
in the garbage disposal,
or put them in a vase?
I started worrying
about flowers withering,
stalks drooping, shriveled
leaves, and dried up petals
falling to their death.
Swiveling around the kitchen
in the lime green padded chair
I noticed the striped yellow wallpaper
matched the crocheted place mats,
the napkin holders, the quilted toaster cover.
I wasn't supposed to touch anything—
her notepads, grocery lists, paper clipped coupons,
the newspaper obituaries of people
she didn't even know marked and highlighted
with a red felt-tipped pen.

Taharah

How beautiful you are, my love, my friend; doves of your eyes looking out
from the thicket of your hair, like two fawns grazing in a field of lilies.
                                                              —Song of Songs

The daughter imagines herself entering the room
through an open window where crocheted curtains
breathe in and out the morning's crisp air, *neshama.*

Faceless women, *chevra kadishra,* long dark tresses
tucked under *mitpachat,* tiny blue flowers dot cotton dresses,
white Sketchers, fingers ringless, their own nails, cleaned,
clipped and unpolished.

In silence, hand washing, water pouring, motioning,
cleaning, cleansing, cloths, more water, towels;
The *chevra* nod to each other and sway, say prayers
for the dressing, the undressing, *misbreberach,* and *mechillah,*
a prayer for peace, *Oseh Shalom.*

The daughter imagines surrounding her mother's body
with golden Jonagolds, a garland of autumn leaves
in place of the cotton cap where wisps of white hair poke through.

The daughter watches in silence like a deer,
from the bracken thicket after sunrise.
She watches as the dragonfly lands on a stalk of wheat,
her own breath suspended in air, like the fly fisherman's line
before it strikes the water's surface.

Below the arms of the women, she smells
the rose milk lotion of her mother's skin,
the vanilla yogurt of her mother' breath.

At home, she waits in her room for the call
from the caregiver, the one that will release
her mother from pain.

A Million Stars

In the center of the stage,
the rabbi spreads his white tasseled
arms, motions us to stand or sit,
sit or stand. Whenever I rise, my itchy wool
stockings fall to my knees. I want my mother's
help, but she sings *Avinu Malkeneiu,* rocking
and bowing. I stare at the backs of women's heads,
black coats with leopard collars, lace pinned
to their stiff white hair. So hot, men's ears redden
like dried apricots. My head rests on the bench,
I gaze at the canopy of stained-glass stars,
shimmering blues, reds, and yellows.
I pray if I count each star, one by one,
forward and backward, side by side,
I can finally go home.

Unleashed

Dear Albania

This is not the stick-sock
         doll you kicked in alleys
with your friends for fun.
         Not the frogs you caught
with your mother's dental floss
         at the canal, deep fried
legs for lunch.

Albania, you haven't any
         flashing crosswalk lights.
Your people run
         like frightened hens,
children holding each other's
         hands—bursting across
the street, zigzagging around darting cars.

Those are no longer your parents
         sitting on their sofa,
watching their dictator, Enver Hoxa,
         who jailed painters for liking Picasso,
and musicians who played the Beatles.

Albania, these are your beaches
         dotted with abandoned
military bunkers—transformed into cafes lit with tiny
         Christmas lights.
Goodbye to your country, your family, toasting *Raki,* and *burek,*
         feta cheese, roasted lamb.
Goodbye to your mother beating the rugs, scrubbing the floor
         on her hands and knees.
Dear Albania, you no longer need your double-headed
         vigilant eagle flag

waving red, black, and white as the ghosts
    of Skanderbeg's flailing hospital gown
cast out of his country,
     wandering moon, rogue star.

I Remember Not Sleeping

I remember lying on a squeaky cot, in a room full of Czech
women, listening to them breathe like lung machines.

I remember steam hissing from radiators, heels clicking down halls.

I remember, on the psychiatric ward, thinking that the patients
were doctors who were there to save me because I was dying.

A flashlight shone in my eyes every two hours during the night,
a needle poked my arm.

Someone always watched me in the shower with a flashlight.

I remember waking up at night to use the bathroom
and seeing Czech nurses watching porn on TV.

I remember having sex with men, multiple men, and women,
but I don't remember feeling anything except sore.

I was never tired. And never hungry.

I got a day pass from the hospital and snuck into a man's car.
We smoked unfiltered Camels and listened to Metallica.

I hated heavy metal, but it felt good to be held.

I remember the doctor asking me if I had been breastfed,
and what it meant to throw stones in glass houses.

I was afraid if I didn't get the answers right, something bad would happen to me. One doctor said sleep deprivation causes mania.

My roommate swallowed a crushed light bulb.

I remember the bitter taste of pills I hid under my tongue.

I remember how good it was to come home—to stretch my legs across my bed, wrap myself in clean, cotton sheets and listen
    to the rain.

Snow fell my last night in Prague before I got on a plane to the
    States.

I wasn't sure I would come back, but I wasn't thinking about that. I'd have to be up for 20 hours or more to get home.

Drug Clinic

From where I sit on the toilet, I count three rolls of fat
hanging over the tech's zebra stretch pants.
"Lift your skirt higher," she says.
She points between my legs,
her nails pink with little gold stars.

I hold the cup under me so long my hand shakes.
It reminds me of the tremor I had
from the meds at the hospital.
My hair fell in clumps in the shower.
Black strands scattered over the white pillows.
The doctor said, "Don't worry. Your body
will adjust." But when he upped my dosage
my arms went rigid like an automaton.
Dustin, the schizophrenic, made fun at me
as I shuffled past him down the hall.
"Whore!" he yelled.

Now the tech stares at me and waits.
The more she stares, the more my hand shakes.
Outside the bathroom, patients smoke cigarettes
and wait their turn.

Rummaging

Off the bus, my mother struts in front
of me in a rush to the bank.
She waves her finger at the teller
counting bills behind the window.
"Where's the chubby one?" she says.
I stand behind her and tug her arm.
"Stop it," she says. She pulls away,
rummaging through her black leather
fanny pack for her driver's license.
I know she won't find it.
"They know me here," she yells.
Behind the window, the manager nods to me.
He says to her: "It's okay, Mrs. Levine."
I turn around and face the security guard,
the taser on his belt. He doesn't flinch.
Has she done this before?
I feel sweat dripping under my arms
and into my bra.
Everything is red and hot,
like the inside of a mouth, screaming.

Because of Poetry

Swiveling in an office chair,
in a shell of a room,
the psych hospital allowed
me to tap tap tap
on an old Mac.
How lucky I was!
Ideas popped out of my head
like cosmic candy.
I tried to tune out
the sounds outside—
a trumpet blasting
the same broken
notes, the choking breath
of the *krekht* clarinet,
32 brass bronze bells
clamoring like a funeral.
A slam against the wall,
shattering plaster,
crumpled bits
on the mucked up floor.
The chuck cluck cluck
of the stiff breasted nurses,
rounding up patients who bobbed
and shuffled for supper.
And the doctor, the conductor
of this disgruntled orchestra
checked and rechecked the clock.
Tucking in his shirt,
he clutched a stack of files

in his sweaty palms,
bowed to the staff
who sat and jeered
behind glass windows.

But I Do Not Need Madness

I have known madness in my bones,
at dinner tables, pot roast, and mashed potatoes.

Small-talking strangers in dim-lit diners drinking cups
of coffee, spreading butter and jam on toast.

I have seen madness in the eerie calm of streets,
around dark corners, anonymous store shutters,

in hospital beds, isolation rooms, old age homes,
where unhinged men fist fight over Bingo.

I've known madness in Shelley, Shuman, Zelda, and Poe,
thieves roaming the streets,

rabid dogs, sniffing sour milk jars
in garbage bins, clawing through cans of beans.

I have seen madness in kindness, open handed crumbs,
curved fingers beckoning kisses, mushy as an overripe peach.

I have known promises of marriage, brides and grooms,
driving off in Ford Fiestas, bodies and hoods

decorated with candied dots, *Just Married!*
toward a desert moon,

howling coyotes, pine and sage, over jagged mountains,
passing roadsides of crosses and corsages,

a sunset so *breathtaking,* the bride rests her head
on the groom's lap and weeps.

Tell Me What It's Like

It's as if my brain traveled
a long way across the Arizona
desert. Dehydrated, worn,
deviled by dirt and sand,
pierced by prickly pear spines.
Left on the road,
rusted, bruised, burned.
A javelina stops to sniff,
snorts, and turns its back.
A strong wind kicks it
like a furless rabbit.
A gray wolf pisses
on it, and a red-tailed
hawk swoops
down, snags
my brain, lifts it
over a fence,
dropping it
into a green pasture
in a small stream
where shade
feels like spring.

Sitting Shiva on Custer Park Hill

I spot a flock of crows
flit from tree to tree.
They *kibitz,* rattle and click,
like a congregation of mourners
trying to find their seats.

I'm sitting *shiva* on Custer Park hill
on the same bench
my mother and I shared
a year ago.

She handed me sliced apples
smeared in honey,
"May we have a happy and healthy
New Year," she said,
her green eyes wide with hunger
after a whole day of fasting
for Yom Kippur.

I noticed her hair had bleached white,
more crow's feet when she smiled;
now she is more beautiful to me
in my memories of her,

like silence in prayer,
from dusk to twilight to dawn
in *Yizkor,* when the rabbi shouts out her name,
shakes the sleep out of my bones.

Stealing Flowers from the Neighbors

No dark sunglasses, no hood over my head,
no scissors, shopping bag slung over my shoulder,

I slide behind bushes, pricked by brambles,
yank and snap, rip and tear.

No worry or rush,
or hush from the birds.

Squirrels, too busy collecting nuts,
don't stop on the lawn to judge.

Dandelion seeds fill the air like dust.
A silent sneeze, a cough caught in my throat,

I crawl under towering weeds
and hedges, wedge myself

between rocks and prickly thorns.
I do not feel the scraping of my knees

or the bee sting, burn of the sun
on my cheeks, heat on my hatless head.

Stealing flowers from the neighbors
I could only think of you in your hospice bed,

your weary head,
waiting for me to appear.

Lilacs

Today, I don't have to be kind. I don't have to return
        your phone calls, shower, comb my hair
When you ask, "yes, she is still dying."

In a quiet room, blanketed by light, a bouquet of lilacs
    droop next to a bruised banana, glass of mango juice,
        vanilla ice cream dripping from a spoon.

"Smell," I gently tousle petals to her nose.
    She shakes her head, turns away.

Her breath, now slow and strained,
        each kiss a whisper, a tiny puff of air,

her mottled, frigid skin
    wafts metallic.

Eyes glassy and blue-green stare at my nose
            "How did you get that bump on your face?"
Her knotted finger peruses its shape.

I lift my mask to kiss
        and kiss the part of her face I hope
            she can still feel.

I stroke her moist hair,

"I am here, Mom. I am here."

My Mother Stays in Bed

"My bed is like a boat," she says.
       "floating down an ancient river,
the current between my toes.
       I hear cries of herons
Long-legged and fierce,
       their razor beaks
pierce flapping fish,
       swallowing them down whole."

I offer her a spoonful of soup
       hold it to her thin, dry lips
but the soup drips down her chin,
       onto her gown.

"I've seen rivers," she says. "I've seen
       fish jump and fifty more fly.
"I've never seen you cry," she tells me,
       holding my hand in hers,
like moss clinging to stone.

Through the Window at the Hospice Center

Mom,

I'm almost finished. Your bills are paid, clothes sorted, books piled in boxes.
I keep finding things—
A birth certificate stuffed between your art prints, your father's death certificate, the place and date when you married, how much I weighed at my birth.
I've been finding twenties in drawers, unopened checks in your mail. I just found your diamond rings and pearl necklaces in the front pocket of your new suitcase. Hair balls under the bed, dust in the white shag carpet, dates scribbled down, newspaper articles clipped.
I took a walk today and found a lilac bush. Like the one outside my window when I was little, the one growing next to the tree with the bird's nest. Do you remember, Mom?
Purple petals in my fingers, I cupped them into my face. Like a bouquet, I wish I could carry that smell over to your window today. *Would you be able to smell them?*
"Smell is one of the things to go when you are dying," the hospice nurse said.
Soon, I will enter your room and hold you in my arms, crawl into your skin. W*e can swim into the ocean, in the sparkling waves, our backs arched, somersaulting, tugging the tide, then letting go.*

Camellia's Bloom

At the hospice center,
Mom lies exhausted in bed,
stares absently through
the sky's broken blue.

The sinews of her limp
arm wrap around my neck,
brittle nails poke my shoulder.

I press my ear to her mouth.
"Am I going to heaven?" she whispers.
I want to gaze into her green eyes,
the two of us—green leaves—
rest our heads on the stem
of camellia's bloom.

I watch her heartbeat so fiercely,
it bulges from her chest.
I leave her room with a handful
of diamond rings, an amber bracelet,
a sample of her favorite perfume.

Out in the common room,
some of the patients are stirring—
classical strings play on the radio,
hard boiled eggs bubble to the pot's surface,
the tv turns itself on.

I watch Magda stuff lilacs, peonies,
and irises into a vase.
"You must have a beautiful garden,"
she smiles, arranges the flowers
as if they are for her.

"Beautiful," she says again,
places the vase in the center
of the kitchen table,
decorated with embroidery.

My Questions for the Hospice Nurse

Why can't I feel my bra on my skin?
Do I put it on first, then my socks?

How do I fry an egg?
When will she stop swallowing? Stop eating?

Why are her toenails and fingernails still growing?

Did I wipe her? Did I wash myself? Did I brush her teeth?
Have I brushed my teeth? Combed my hair?

When was the last time I went outside, fed the squirrels, really
listened to the birds?
Why are there keys in my hand, glasses on my face, milk still
sitting on the table?

Why did I pee in my pants in the middle of the night? Is her diaper
full?

Is she here or somewhere in the past?

> We're swimming in the pool at the Y.
> I'm spinning around the kitchen table wearing my pink
tutu.
> She's teaching me how to skip behind the supermarket.

She's tracing the wall with her finger. Is she drawing, painting,
teaching? What does she
see on that blank, white wall?

Did I give her the right pills, enough pills? Did I take my pills, or did I forget them again?

When the rabbi with the Invisalign braces came to visit, he said there are no new prayers. Is this God's will? *Her* will?

Unleashed

Since my mother died, I haven't been able to read.
The words on the page blur
like a child blowing ink through a straw,
the image, a black splotch with branches
of tiny arms, hands, and feet.

My mother used to teach me art
on our back porch—
a can of turpentine, scattered tubes of thick paint,
dirty rags, brushes in a pickle jar.
Open window, a curtain shift,
a clothesline of pinned white
cotton sheets.

I used to watch
her tanned tennis arms
press and pull the iron
along our damp clothes,
steam sounded like a sighing dog
waiting to be unleashed.

Frostbitten

I wrap my sadness around
me like my green puffy jacket
in frozen New York winters.
My sadness stands alone
in our backyard
of our red brick house
and Christmas-less fir trees.
Lonely toboggans and skis
lean against our musty garage walls.
My sadness stuffs snow
into my new Apollo moon boots,
pushes wind against me, stings
my cheeks, burns my ears, numbs my toes.
My sadness scrapes and digs
car windshields, carves marks
from shovels, stamps mud
footprints in crusted over
snow. My sadness melts like
rock salt on our street,
uncovers scars from
our bleeding cherry tree.
My sadness sounds like
our white-haired landlady's
accent, thick as my mother's
black bread spread with
limburger cheese.
I feel my sadness in bumps
of blood moving through my wrist.
Thinking of you, Mom
is like trying to
to rescue a snowflake
from the palm of my glove.

Weeding

Rocks crumble under my shoes,
leaves crunch, dead grass crowds
around me. At any moment,
I might lose my ground.
Braless in my t-shirt and jeans,
I kick and whack,
yank and snap. With the back
of my hand, I wipe sweat off my neck.
Weeding is like marriage—
push-pull
right-wrong
healthy-rotten.
What you bother to take out
strains the muscles
and returns the next day.
I listen to a crow
on the street wire
tell me the strangeness
of myself.
I whisper the things
I cannot change.
At last,
I chop the heads off
yellow weeds
and leave the rest to seed.

Reading in the Dark

Tonight, I tried to read a book before bed
but I couldn't see the book
or anything else.
The lightbulb in my lamp
had gone out.
After fifteen years,
imagine that.
I didn't know light bulbs
could last that long.
In the store, you held the lamp,
and asked me,
Is this the one?
I said, it reminds me of a crane,
not the one that catches fish
but the machine that swings
and lifts its heavy arms
lowering its weight to the ground.
Sometimes, at night, when it's quiet,
I take long walks in my neighborhood
gaze at the sky's bright lights
and wonder if you see them too.

Remembering Her Less

My mother
rocked us in her chair,
untangling my thick braids,
brushing my hair until
it covered my shoulders.

Lately, I've been
forgetting small things,
even her voice
is starting to fade,
as in her old age,
those songs she sings
but cannot name.

Postscript

One Life

I am a ram without a horn.
      A horn without a mouthpiece.
A mouthpiece without a King,
      a King without commandments.
Commandments without a mountaintop.
      I am a mountaintop without towering trees,
a myrtle without birds.
      Without birds, I am silence
Silently, your voice echoes my name.
      You are the rain covering the desert plain
droplet by droplet you fall on everything.

Work Cited

Schwartz, Delmore, "In Dreams Become Responsibilities," *In Dreams Begin Responsibilities and Other Stories* (New Directions, 1978)

About the Author

Sherri Levine is the author of the chapbook *In These Voices,* published in 2018 by The Poetry Box. She is the recipient of the 2019 Lois Cranston Memorial Poetry Prize and was awarded Poet's First Prize in the Oregon Poetry Association biannual contest in 2017. Her poetry has appeared in *Poet Lore, The Timberline Review, CALYX, CIRQUE, Clackamas Literary Review, Driftwood Press, The Jewish Literary Journal, Mizmor Anthology, Worcester Review,* and elsewhere. She served as Co-Editor of *Voice Catcher-A Journal of Women's Voices and Visions* and has taught English-as-a-Second Language for over two decades at colleges and universities. She was recently accepted for a residency at the Mineral School. Sherri hosts *Head for the Hills*—a monthly poetry reading series and open mic. She lives in Portland, Oregon.